Jonah's Judgment

—ɯ—

A parable of judgment and justice

Robert W Foster

Also by Robert W. Foster

Michael's Eyes: The life and times of a man born blind

*"It is not good to have zeal
without knowledge,
nor to be hasty and miss
the way."*

Proverbs 19:2

Contents

Foreword

The story of Jonah and the city of Ninevah is a parable of judgment and justice. It is about the determination of one man to see judgment brought against a wicked society in contrast to God's plan of mercy following contrition and confession.

Jonah is one of the most recognizable names of the Old Testament. People who know little more than the Ten Commandments know about Jonah and the whale. Unfortunately, that is the limit of most people's understanding of the story; it is always *Jonah-and-the-whale*. The account of a man being regurgitated from the belly of a whale after three days may be understood as myth or miracle and is impressive in its vivid imagery. But it is not the message of the book.

The popular concept of the Old Testament God in our modern, doubting culture is that of an angry, vengeful, punishing God. The God of Jonah, on the other hand, is determined to forgive a whole community their collective guilt if they will repent.

Jonah is a man called by God to deliver a message to an evil society. The message was to be a call to repentance but Jonah could not accept the possibility that through repentance, those wicked people might be forgiven and saved from the destruction earned by their sin and guilt. This parable of justice and judgment is not intended as an expiation of Jonah, a stubborn and uncompromising accuser.

The book of Jonah in the Old Testament canon is one more demonstration of God's desire to bring His creation back into communion with Himself by offering forgiveness in the face of certain judgment. It is a demonstration of the willingness of God to forgive in contrast to one man's determination to condemn.

—ᙡ—

Introduction

Spread in front of me is Nineveh, that *great city*. I, Jonah, await its destruction; this *great city* will be reduced to rubble, its leaders burned, its people killed. I wait to see dust rise from the ground to the sky, its buildings crushed. I will be satisfied only when I hear cries of anguish from its people and their beasts. I hold no pity for its families; even the children must feel the wrath of a just and righteous God. All are guilty: those who have celebrated their idolatry, those who have reveled in their debauchery, those who have made graft and corruption a normal way of doing business, those who have claimed entitlement to every source of pleasure. All are guilty. All born into that ugly world have inherited their parents' guilt; they, too, are deserving of death from youngest to oldest. Therefore the Lord will inflict punishment on Nineveh.

My whole life has been devoted to teaching righteousness and justice. Not only is God's law well known to us Hebrews; logic should be enough to convince all men that only in harmony and peace can they hope for happiness in this life. But these people have built their society on a premise of strength and superiority over their neighbors. They have enslaved others for their own leisure; they have brought home wealth taken from the innocents they have conquered, building the opulence and wonder of their own *great city*. But that has not been enough for them. Having achieved such wealth they have turned on the weakest members of their own society who in turn steal from their brothers.

Men and women in this *great city* treat each other and themselves as do the beasts. There is no sanctity in marriage, no stability nor loyalty in families. Incest is common, bestiality normal, men with men, women with women; they have no shame. The Lord has said, *"I will put an end to lewdness in the Land."*

The young lack respect for their elders; they scorn their parents. The guilt of this city is a stench rising to the heavens, a stench repulsive to the God who gave them life. It is only right and just that God should crush them now.

My fear is that He may not.

I did not ask to come here. The word of the Lord came to me: *"Go to the great city of Nineveh and preach against it, because its wickedness has come up before me."* In fact, I resisted with all my strength the notion that I should bring warning to this people. They do not deserve the right to repentance and, in any case, from my observations they will never heed the warning and ask to be spared. Nor should they be spared. God's law is as He gave it exclusively to us, His chosen people, not to be abridged or amended out of some delicate sense of pity for this *great city*. They have shown no pity nor should they receive any.

My role for more than 40 years has been to bring God's law to His people, scattered from the Great Sea in the West to the fertile crescent of the Tigris and Euphrates in the East; and from Ur of the Chaldeans in the south to Aleppo and Carchemish in the North. The Hebrews know the Law well enough; they merely need me to remind them from time to time. But I am not accustomed to bringing God's words to a heathen people and I have no standing with the Gentiles whereby they should listen to me. Nor is judgment mine to mete out; judgment belongs to the Lord and He must bring judgment in the form of His wrath upon this people.

My fear is that He may not.

And so I wait.

When the message first came to me that I should go to Nineveh, "that great city" in the Lord's words, to preach against it, I rejected the notion. In the first place, to preach against such a people would be an exercise in futility, and to what purpose? To convince them of their sin that they might repent, mend their ways and follow God's laws? And should they do all that, would they be forgiven? Will they be able to go back in time and undo the shame they have brought on themselves and the misery they have inflicted upon others? Can they now, at this late date, reverse their sin? Is there any penance great enough? If so, where is justice to be found if such wickedness may be forgiven? Why, then, should I go into that city of debauchery and announce a warning?

In the second place, if I were to enter that dark and evil city in order to paint for them a picture of their perfidy, would the mob not seize me, beat me, torture me and finally kill me? Should I suffer such humiliation and pain for an impossible venture? This could not be God's will for me! Wherever this crazy idea came from I drove it from my mind, determined to go nowhere near the Assyrian city of Nineveh – and to flee as far as possible from the presence of God and this message.

—∞—

I

Judgment

Who can understand such a people as these Ninevites? I, Jonah, know their history; it is a history of war, conquest and defeat. I know that 700 years ago the Hurrians became powerful in northern Mesopotamia, that area between the great rivers Tigris and Euphrates. Early nomadic people first developed agriculture there and began to settle into communities. The Hurrians founded the kingdom of Mittani in northern Mesopotamia, spreading their influence and power west towards the Great Sea until coming into conflict with Egypt under Tuthmosis I.

For the next hundred years there was conflict between the two powers, pushing each other back and forth over the land by the sea from Tyre to Alleppo until a cynical alliance was formed under Tuthmose IV when Mittani was threatened by the Hittites in the north and a resurgence of the Assyrians in the east.

The alliance was little help to Mittani when the Egyptian pharaoh, Akhenaten, became more interested in matters close to home. King Suppiluliumas of the Hittites built his strength in the region, finally sacking Mittani's capital, Washukanni. Such is the futility of alliances among godless powers.

The traditional history tells us that when the Egyptians regained control over Canaan, Pharaoh Ramses II made war on the Hittites but Muwatallis II of the Hittites defeated Ramses' forces in a great chariot battle at Qadesh, just north of Biblos and Damascus. Hittite control now extended down to Damascus. The two empires confronted each other until the Hittites became more concerned about Assyrian expansion to their east. The Assyrian King

Ashuruballit 1 had taken Nineveh and the surrounding area from the failing Mittani kingdom. One hundred years later, the Assyrian king Tukulti-Ninurta 1 fought the Hittites with success extending his reach from Washukanni in the north to Ur in the south, an infamous Realm that lasted until Tukulti-Ninurta, after a nearly 40 year reign, was assassinated by his own rebellious people.

The Hittites were finally overcome by a people apparently from Thrace, known as the Phrygians. And the Egyptians were attacked by a mysterious people from the sea, whom they drove out only to see them settle in Canaan where they became known as Philistines. At about that time our own people, the Hebrews, were being lead by God into Canaan where they would take up a peaceful residence forever. But conflict continued in Mesopotamia with the Assyrian king, Tiglath-Pileser 1, fighting off a variety of invaders including nomadic Arameans who forced their way into the region, boldly building their own settlements and reducing the Assyrian empire to a limited area around Ashur and Nineveh as it is, essentially, in this age.

The history of these peoples, from Egypt to Mesopotamia, alternately invading and being invaded, slaying and being slain, demonstrates perfectly how members of a godless society (even worse, a society of many gods) must repeatedly fail in their attempt to live and survive among themselves. With such a history it is little wonder that today the people of Nineveh are fallen into total depravity.

"Let the evil of the wicked come to an end," in the words of our great King David.

I turn my back on such a people; I shake the dust of their world from my feet and consign them to exist in their own filth until a righteous God shall cause the destruction of their city as He has warned.

—m—

II

Flight

It is nearly impossible for a man of principle to hold conflicting convictions. It seemed that I had been given clear instruction to go to Nineveh and warn the city of destruction unless the people repented of their collective sin. But I also believe firmly in the principle that deliberate sin deserves certain death. I wanted no part in a venture that could, however unlikely, subvert justice in the case of Nineveh, its leaders and its people. Nor could I believe that God would place me in such a dilemma. I agonized for days and sleepless nights. I paced. I fasted. I begged for clarity; surely, I had misunderstood the message.

I determined it finally to be prudent to turn my back on the situation. The solution was to put as much distance between myself and that evil city as possible, that I might not, in my confusion, follow an obviously wrong impulse. Nineveh was several days travel east, so I turned my face to the west, which meant boarding a ship at Joppa headed out on the Great Sea to Tarshish, the ancient trading port. The ship that I chose was an ungainly shallow draft vessel of laid-up oaken timbers, with a ragged cloth sail hanging from rugged spars that were without grace but appeared adequate to the job. The captain, a short, thick-bodied character who matched his boat for homely strength, was unaccustomed to carrying passengers. His usual freight was rough-cut lumber or slabs of marble to be shipped in one direction and ballast on the return, plus whatever odd assortments of goods might be seeking transport. The ship, I noticed, was equipped with crude oarlocks and long sweep oars stowed in the bilge section, though I could not imagine his crew providing much headway for such a massive blunt object plowing through seawater.

For the crew were not young men; grizzled gray, they were short and bent from long years of heavy labor. They moved around in the boat on bare feet that were scarred and callused from jamming into bollards and being crushed under freight and equipment. Their toes were bent and misshapen and often missing; their hands, too, showed the wear and tear of their occupation. (I am a keen observer of the meanest occupations of the uneducated.) Fingers were missing quite commonly, but it is a curious fact that though a sailor may have fewer than ten fingers, he is never short of a thumb. A sailor may function with only two or three fingers on one hand but if a thumb is severed or crushed or yanked from its socket, he is unable to grasp a rope or pull an anchor; such a man is useless aboard a boat and is quickly put ashore. For a laborer a thumb is as important as an arm or a leg. A working man without both his thumbs has little prospect of employment and is reduced to begging in order to live. Thumb-less or God-less, such a man's prospects are bleak.

I pitied them their brutish lives while they boasted of exploits on shore the night before, as they cast off from the pier. But they were not Hebrews; I could not lecture them on the one God and His Law of purity, obedience and the fruits of a sinless life. It was true, was it not, that I was fleeing from just such an encounter with a lost people who denied the one real God in favor of their many false gods of wood and stone.

There were no cabins or living quarters on board this boat. The men slept on piles of hempen rope and hawsers. The captain had reserved for himself a small corner at the bow of the ship, but I doubted he actually slept there; he seemed always fully alert to the circumstances of sea, ship and crew, and when not steering the craft by its clumsy looking tiller arrangement, he would be prowling about inspecting everything in his domain, muttering his discontent with the general disorder of the craft. Once underway he was king as well as captain; his whole world was contained between the prow and stern of that sturdy craft and the crew were his subjects. There seemed no question but that all our lives were in his hands once we were at sea.

I was assigned space deep below deck alongside odd lengths of lumber where I could store my kit. I had brought a single canvas bag that I carried on my back by loops of leather cording. This and its jumbled contents provided all the bedding I would enjoy during my self-imposed exile. My crude quarters reeked of bilge water, rotting wood and unwashed bodies. The accommodations might be meager but so was the fare I had paid for my passage, so I could hardly complain. I wondered what, if any, food I might be served; as things developed I had no opportunity to learn. We sailed from Joppa as the sun began its rise in the east; I barely had time to stow my gear as the crew cast off from the dock. I was exhausted less from my long trek to Joppa than from the turmoil of my indecision and the conflict in my heart and mind concerning Nineveh. How could I run from what seemed to be God's purpose, but how could I betray the principle of justice He had clearly laid down for me, and to which I had faithfully devoted my life?

I arranged my bedding and quickly fell into a deep sleep before the sun's orb was more than half above the horizon. With the creaking of the ship's ancient timbers, the growlings of the crew at their labors and the gentle rocking of the ungainly ship as it moved through the waves, I was lulled into a deep sleep that lasted through the day and late into the evening. Rarely am I able to enjoy such a dreamless rest; my nights are more normally invaded by images and messages that leave no doubt about the role I am assigned in this life. But this night held no visitation. It was as though my decision to run far from Nineveh and my responsibility there, had been approved and endorsed by God. I think that I probably smiled to myself in my sleep with satisfied relief from my burden. It was as though I had been vindicated in my clear reasoning. Had I time to think about it, I might have compared myself to Abraham who was tested and found faithful.

Instead, late that night, I was awakened abruptly by the captain who was shouting down at me: Did I not care that the ship was in peril? Could I do nothing but sleep while he and the crew fought to save us all?

I rose to the sounds of howling wind, thrashing waves and the captain in a near panic. While I slept, the weather had changed suddenly into a storm that threatened to wreck the ship. I climbed from the hold and found bedlam on the heaving deck. I stood, bewildered for a moment, trying to support myself on the stout walking stick I carried everywhere. The sea was in turmoil, waves surging into the ship from every direction. There was no order to the roiling sea; it was as if the howling wind blew from every point of the compass. Everything that was not fastened securely was thrashing about: gear and goods banging into bulwarks, tools bouncing off the bulkheads. The four crewmen were struggling with the long oars and I at last understood that the oars were less for making progress than for trying to maintain the ship's heading into the giant waves, lest we be broadsided and roll over. Adding to the din, the great rudder at the stern was under attack by the following seas, making the tiller a deadly weapon as it whipped back and forth, threatening anyone within its reach.

The captain was still shouting at me. He knew that I was a Hebrew and challenged me to "call upon your God" to deliver lest we perish. The crew had decided that someone on board had the 'evil eye' and was responsible for this unexpected calamity. It was not difficult to see that they suspected me, a stranger who had never been aboard in the past, while in the past such a storm had never overtaken them. They had cast lots to learn which of us was the source of this evil. The lots, of course, pointed to me. I should not have been surprised to discover wisdom among a godless group of unschooled sailors, even in their superstition. For it was suddenly obvious to me that I, in my rebellion against God, had brought His wrath on me and everyone around me. Meanwhile, as I confronted my own perfidy, the crew were calling out to me from their labors, "Who are you? What is your business here? Where are you from – what place, what people?" So, in my fear and shame, I told them my story, even as the storm continued, so that I had to speak in the raised voice I usually use in my public preaching. For once I had an audience with full attention, clutching at each of my words as though my speech alone might save them. As they labored at the oars, I cried out:

"I am a Hebrew, and I worship the Lord, the God of heaven, who has made the sea and the dry land." I told them of my assignment to Nineveh and my refusal, and they understood, finally, that I had fled from the presence of my God. One of the crew called out, "How can we deal with you to calm the sea? It is getting worse!"

How often in life is a man brought face to face with his own arrogance? Why must a man of my learning and exalted position be found out by his spiritual and intellectual inferiors? And where would I find the courage to do what was obviously required of me? Instead I put the burden on them to betray all ethics of seamanship.

"Throw me overboard and the sea will be calm for you; it is because of me that this great tempest is upon you!" They would not, at first, and instead struggled to row the ship back to shore, but without success. It shamed me to find that those whom I had pitied for their brutish lives had an even greater pity for me.

God's rage continued in ever greater force, making the men still more desperate. They cried out,

"We are begging, O God; we do not want to die because of this man's life. We don't want his blood on our hands, but you are the Lord and all of this is according to Your pleasure." No words could be more gratifying to a preacher than this confession of belief, even said under duress. For all of life is duress, and it is often duress that brings men to a true confession of belief. Those were my final rueful thoughts as I was cast into the sea.

III

Survival

What happened to me in the sea is still a mystery to me. I know that I was enveloped by the waves that churned above and around me. I know, too, that I fought for my life even as I realized I had forfeited any hope of living because of my rebellious rejection of God's will. Eventually the sea calmed around me though the ship was long out of my sight. I struggled for a time on the surface and for a longer time submerged in that dark realm of death. The words of the Psalmist came to me in my despair:

> *"What profit is there in my death, if I go down to this watery Pit? Will*
> *the dust praise You or proclaim Your faithfulness?"*

Was it presumptuous of me to challenge God with these words, as though my life was the only evidence of his greatness? Yes, presumption and arrogance were the first and greatest of man's sins.

But in those hours I had no other argument except to plead my case. Even following my denial of His will for me, even in my shame, and especially at the point of death, I believed in my role as God's singular prophet. As I fought to stay afloat, I argued my case.

Now I try to remember what happened next, but there is only darkness. Perhaps I became delirious in my exhaustion or maybe God in His mercy removed all consciousness from me and bore me up or he might even have employed the beasts of the sea to save me. I don't know what happened, I only know that after what must have been a very long time in the sea (we had sailed for many hours out of Joppa before the storm struck and were far from land), I began to regain my senses. Soon I heard the sound of surf breaking on a shore, my feet found the earth, and I staggered out and fell upon dry land as though expelled from the sea. Again, I recalled the words of the Psalmist:

"You brought me up, O Lord, from the dead. You restored my life as I was going down to the grave."

I knew then that I would go to Nineveh.

—◊—

IV

Nineveh

Once again the message came clearly to me. I was to go there and cry against the city:

"Yet 40 days and Nineveh shall be overthrown."

Now I began to see God's plan. He intended to destroy the city but would first give fair warning. The city would ignore the message, probably even laugh in scorn at such simplicity, and at last, God willing, it would perish. And I would be vindicated. All I had to do was march about the city with my message, a matter of three days journey from end to end. I believed that in the 40 days God had promised them, I would be able to bring the warning to most of the doomed population, after which, I would go and watch from afar.

On my arrival at Nineveh I entered through the gates unchallenged and ignored. Around me was the incongruity of a rich community peopled by a society of beggars and thieves, businessmen and bankers, prostitutes and politicians. The citizens moved through the streets furtively, heads down, eyes fixed on the ground before them. It was as though each person was a fugitive who might at any moment be seized, or perhaps what I was seeing was the fright-filled outlook of people subject to assault and attack. It seemed that everyone viewed his neighbor as a potential robber or rapist.

"The poor are shunned even by their neighbors, but the rich have many friends."

I walked toward the heart of the city until I came to a busy intersection of streets. I stood at the corner and delivered my warning in my strongest preacher's voice while trembling with an anticipation of violent reaction from the people. "Repent, for in 40 days the one true God will destroy this wicked city!" Then I recited Solomon's proverb:

"The Lord detests men of perverse heart but He delights in those whose ways are blameless. Be sure of this: The wicked will not go unpunished, but those who are righteous will go free."

I was surprised by the passive reaction. Some looked at me as though I was a crazy man, smirked, and walked on by. Some young boys stood for a moment, laughed and called out, "You said it, old man!" A few people quickly crossed the street to get away from my voice, shaking their heads, muttering, I suppose, that something ought to be done about such a public spectacle. Others became more vocal, shouting back at me, trying to drown out my voice. It was clear to me that these people did not want to hear about their fallen state; they were satisfied with their own pitiful lives and welcomed no contradiction. But there was no violence against me.

For the next few days as I continued, few crowds gathered, but once in a while I would notice a man or a woman standing there with a slight frown as though troubled by my words. I had expected that some would take umbrage at my boldness and throw a stone or two. That didn't happen, but I knew there would be many more days of this and I continued with some anxiety for my safety. On the other hand, I was on God's mission and He had saved me from a watery death precisely so that I could participate in His plan to rid the world of this scourge. These thoughts gave me courage to carry on. The risk that they might repent and be forgiven by a generous God was far from my mind now.

On the following days I continued my journey into and through the city with the same message, except that instead of 40 days it became 39, then 38, 37 and so on. Wherever I found crowds or small groups of people I would stop and begin with my speech. As time went on, I admit, I became bolder. I made my message more direct, accusing the people of collective sin and a personal responsibility for their sins. I called out about God's displeasure with the habits and practices of the people. I became explicit in my accusations, expecting violent reactions from the mobs, but still, that did not happen. Instead, strangely, as many people began to listen to me as those who rejected my message.

One day as I was warning of destruction of the city in 33 days, a man approached and asked to speak privately with me. We stepped to the side of the street and he introduced himself to me. He was a member of a weavers' guild, an association of professional weavers who met periodically to discuss costs and wages and their relations with the city leaders. He said that several of their members had heard my message and wanted to know more about me. Where was I from? Whom did I represent? And most importantly, what was the source of this disturbing message I was broadcasting about the city? Would I meet with them? Of course I would, and we made an appointment for the next evening.

—⟡—

V

The Weavers

The Weavers' Guild was not a large group but seemed, at first, to be a sober, intelligent gathering of businessmen. The evening began with a generous meal of fish, rice, bread and a local wine which some of the members enjoyed a bit too much, in my opinion. Their discussion centered on the conditions of their trade, like workers' wages and the cost of materials (too high) and profits (too low). But the main issue of interest to these men seemed to be the burden of the government over them: high taxes and too much regulation of their business. Taxes were high, yes, but worse than that was the "tribute" they were required to pay. I did not understand this issue at first, but it soon became clear to me that they were making payments to certain government inspectors beyond the usual fees and taxes.

I was witnessing a casual discussion on the subject of graft and corruption, not especially surprising to me for I had full knowledge of the venality of the people and institutions of Nineveh. What did distress me was learning that the "tribute" was to encourage the city's inspectors to overlook the working conditions in the weavers' shops. Were the workers' hours long, and the conditions unsafe and unsanitary? Well, the workers were lucky to have jobs in these difficult times. Were there crippling accidents to men working with the looms? The men were clumsy and careless. One member described an incident in which a worker lost his right arm while moving heavy equipment. "That accident cost me several hours of production while we disentangled the fellow and got the men back to work again." There was no report of the injured man's fate. It was only right, they agreed, that the city's inspectors should tend to more important matters and it was highly unjust that they must be paid tribute to leave the weavers alone to ply their trade without government interference.

The discussion turned to a certain contract the weavers hoped to enter into with the government. Apparently the king's soldiers were to be clothed in uniforms made by the weavers after a bidding process in which the local members of this guild were in competition with a group from the nearby city of Ashur. It could be a lucrative piece of business and it was important that these men know what the competition would bid for the work, that their own bid not be so high that they lose the award, nor so low as to limit their profits from the work. Now the strategy was to identify that person in the king's offices who might accept "tribute" for providing such information. I was witnessing graft and corruption in practice as though this was a normal means of doing business.

It was also clear to me that these weavers represented a major industry of Nineveh and that they felt privileged to enjoy special treatment from the government, even if they must contribute to certain key officials in a position to regulate their trade, taxes and the working conditions of the employees. In fact their enterprise was a major element in the economy of Nineveh; they were important to the city and the city was important to them. I began to understand why my message of impending doom might be especially alarming to these men. If my message was true it would mean great loss to them. If false, my message might still cause panic in the community, distracting the workers from their labors, interrupting the smooth flow of the operations.

Finally I was introduced to the group and invited to tell my story. I proceeded carefully. I described myself as a Hebrew whose role it was to carry God's message to His people as prophet and teacher. I explained that we Hebrews had known the one true God for many years. (I did not, out of an instinct for prudent diplomacy, point out to them that we were God's Chosen People.) I had been instructed to come specifically to Nineveh to warn the residents of God's displeasure with their way of life with the warning that if the city did not repent He would cause its destruction. One of the younger members interrupted me to ask what was wrong with their way of life. Again I was careful in my answer but as I warmed to the subject, I reverted to form as the severe preacher, becoming more colorful, even outraged, in a description of the vile practices of the people of Nineveh, including the dearth of ethics among this very group.

"We have a proverb I said,

> "'There is deceit in the hearts of those who plot evil, but joy for those who promote peace.'

And another:

> " 'Misfortune pursues the sinner, but prosperity is the reward of the righteous.' "

After several minutes of this I stopped, impressed with my own oratory but suddenly worried I had gone too far. The room remained silent for what seemed like a long time while I expected an enraged response to my tirade. Once again, I was surprised. One who seemed the leader of the Guild stood and thanked me politely for taking the time to speak to them. They would need more time to digest my words and decide what, if anything, they should do in response. Realizing I had been politely excused, I left quickly, expecting not to hear from the Weavers' Guild again.

—w—

VI

A New Strategy

Later, when I had time to think about my hour with the weavers I remembered the young man's question, "What is wrong with our way of life?" At first I took his question as a kind of challenge as though to say, *where did I get the right to enter their city and criticize their lifestyle?* On reflection, I realized that there may be more behind the question. Perhaps what was missing was their lack of an ethical law.

Without ethics how are a people to know the difference between right and wrong?

I had always thought it was self-evident, that nature itself would show man through logic, that to live in harmony with one another was the only way to achieve peace. Perhaps because they had not been told how to live, they lived however they wished and wished only to please themselves. Once again I realized the miracle of grace: that God had chosen the Hebrews and had revealed His law to us as a unique people, blessed above all others, favored with knowledge of His law that set us apart from other peoples. At that moment I bent my knee and praised God, thanking Him that I was a Hebrew and not one of these ignorant and doomed Ninevites.

So I changed my strategy. In my public pronouncements I no longer began with a litany of these peoples' sins. Instead I began with the assertion that, contrary to their beliefs, there was only one God who was Creator of all things and Master of the Universe. I went on to the major points of God's Law. I told them that firstly, God wanted men to love and respect Him and secondly that God wanted men to love one another. (At this point I would explain God's love in contrast to the hideous carnal love practiced in Nineveh, men with men and women with women.) Then I stressed that in God's eyes it is wrong for people to hate and kill each other, steal from one another, each one coveting what the other had — even including another man's wife. I told them that God expected children to love and honor their parents, and by the way, that parents had continuing responsibilities for their children's lives. Only then would I point out to them how they failed at every point of the Law, giving explicit examples of their sin.

"You must understand," I said to them, "that the one great God is not only a righteous God, but a vengeful and unforgiving God." I introduced this new strategy in my preaching when there were only 28 days remaining until the destruction of Nineveh.

—⅏—

VII

Nineveh's Mothers

I began to feel real satisfaction in the role God had assigned me, and pride for my performance in carrying out His wishes. I believed that the strategy I had developed was what God had wanted all along. I was bringing God's Law, His ethical standards, to these people for the first time in their history. The people of Nineveh would not go to their collective destruction without an understanding of their sin according to God's Law and both God and I would be free of remorse, knowing we had provided them all they needed for an honest repentance and delivery from the sure destruction awaiting them. At the same time, I felt a recurring dread that God might forgive these people should they repent, and that worst of all, it would be my powerful preaching that might bring them to repentance.

Two days later as I continued my public delivery of God's warning, I was approached again, this time by a group of middle-aged women. They, too, had questions for me so we stood there in a public square as they ranged before me like an appointed delegation. It turned out that most of these women were wives abandoned by their husbands while some were merely unwed mothers. They had heard about my claim that God assigns responsibility to children as well as to parents. I had quoted the Proverbs,

> "'A good man leaves an inheritance for his children's children, but a sinner's wealth is stored up for the righteous', and,
> 'He who spares the rod hates his son, but he who loves him is careful to discipline him,' and again,
> 'A wise son brings joy to his father, but a foolish man despises his mother.'"

"Explain this, please," one woman said. "Does it work among you Hebrews? What must we do to ensure that our children will care for us in our old age? Must we and the fathers of our children continue to recognize this principle even long after our husbands have abandoned us? And should our ex-husbands actually remember us, the forgotten and abandoned companions of their youthful years, into our old age when we are no longer desirable to them?" These women were not hearing the message. Instead of recognizing their own sins and the approaching peril, they were recounting the sins committed against them by the unfaithful men of their lives; what they wanted was relief from their hopeless misery. The fate of the city was the least of their concerns. I was reminded of another proverb:

"The fathers eat sour grapes and the children's teeth are on edge."

I could see no way to deal with such social-cultural issues, standing on a street corner, confronted by these resentful women. As Solomon said, *"A wise woman builds her house, but with her own hands the foolish one tears hers down."*

I could only say to them that with a mere 25 days until the sure destruction of their city, they could not hope to reverse the godless traditions of their history. Their concern should be reconciliation with the one true God through repentance and a city-wide plea for forgiveness and mercy. I left them to consider these harsh words, realizing I could never satisfy their needs.

That night I began to question my mission and my attitude toward the people of Nineveh. For it was not just a city of institutions and traditions. It was a collection of individual persons, each with their own hopes and fears, wants and needs, aspirations and disappointments - people like the mistreated workers and the despairing mothers. Should they perish along with the rest of the city? Is there not a degree of guilt, some not as bad as others? Must all perish?

But I was reminded that the earthquake and tornado make no distinction. The whirlwind does not sift the noble from the ignoble. God is inflexible in His standards; He must stamp out sin from before His eyes and He is full of wrath and will wreak vengeance on Nineveh in all its sin. In the Psalmist's words,

"The Gentiles are sunk down in the pit that they made; and their foot is caught in the net which they hid."

On reflection, I knew my role: I must warn them - but the city must fall.

—ᴡ—

VIII

Nineveh's Priests

In the following days, I was approached by several groups complaining about the circumstances of life in their city, pointing blame at various institutions, trying to absolve themselves of the guilt I had documented so persuasively. Workers complained of low wages and long, slave-like hours; the lower classes were treated unfairly, they said, while the upper classes became wealthy as a result of their back-breaking labors.

At the same time, the wealthy complained bitterly of exorbitant taxes laid upon them. Everyone believed their king and his government abused them, taking their young men to serve as soldiers and their young women to serve in their courts. Yet no one could see the extent of his own guilt, and all of this crying and complaining only spurred me on to more accusations against them collectively with my prediction that the city and all in it would perish now in only 21 days.

Finally I received a visitation by the priests of the city, *those who serve wood and stone.* I had been expecting them since the day I arrived in Nineveh. As I had anticipated, they were puffed up with importance and the assurance of their position. They began by accusing me of blasphemy, sedition and heresy against their gods. They thundered against me and my message; retribution would pour down upon me and I would be swallowed up in my insolence.

I heard them out in silence until their fury was spent. I was emboldened by the wise old proverb,

> *"The Lord detests the sacrifice of the wicked, but the prayer of the upright pleases Him."*

I calmly pointed out to them that their gods were a false invention of their own imagination and were powerless against me because I stood in the light and power of the one true God who had sent me with a warning for the city of Nineveh.

"But my message is not for you, vile corruptors of all that is true and pure," I said. "It is for the city and its people, who will understand the reasons for the destruction that is about to be brought on them in only 20 days '*by the Lord's mighty hand and outstretched arm and with outpoured wrath.*'

"As for you and your gods, I challenge you – at this moment – call down upon my head the retribution you speak of! Call upon your impotent gods right now to defeat me.

"I am waiting - what, no response?"

The priests walked away muttering among themselves.

I heard no more from the religious institutions of Nineveh.

IX

A Public Response

During the next few days there began an energetic debate at nearly every level of society. I was invited to speak to more civic groups until finally I was scheduled to address large audiences assembled in the city's central park. These sessions were followed by public demonstrations in which people began to demand that the government do something before it was too late. The city's security forces started to pay attention to these gatherings and had apparently been instructed to maintain order at any cost. One day, as I began my usual presentation by announcing that in only 17 days Nineveh would be destroyed, the large crowd that had assembled became restive. There was muttering, then some shouting by impatient young men for the king to do something, followed by pushing and shoving, then fighting, until finally the assembly broke into an uproar. The security services moved in with their batons and truncheons. I could hear cries of protest, then screams of pain. When it was over I could see the dead and injured everywhere I looked. I felt no pity for them then, only vindication in my righteous anger toward these hopeless people.

However, the public mood suddenly changed and I was, once again, surprised by this turn of events. Small groups began meeting in homes to discuss the approaching destruction of the city. These groups began, spontaneously, to pray to "the Unknown God" for pity and delivery. The small groups grew to ever larger congregations meeting in public where men began to plead with their neighbors to fall down in worship and supplication. It became, astonishingly, a community-wide practice, spreading through the city like a storm. When

I learned that the weavers and their workers had abandoned their work to join the protest, I realized that something special was taking place in Nineveh.

This practice spread until finally even the king and his court had to take notice. An emissary approached me with a long list of questions regarding my pronouncements. I was instructed to appear the next day before the king to explain myself and my mission. This, I was sure, would be the culmination of all my work for the past 32 days. I expected to be arrested, possibly deported, maybe killed. My earlier fears for my own safety returned; I forgot all about God's preservation of my life so that I could carry out His wishes. The city may be doomed, but so, certainly, was I.

X

A Summons

My audience with the king began with a review of the questions posed to me the previous day. These were all about my background and credentials, and the source of my information regarding Nineveh's imminent destruction. Who was I to make such a claim, going about with warnings of destruction, stirring up the city, causing demonstrations and riots? Who had sent me; who were my masters? Were the Egyptians behind this? Was this a threat of invasion and war?

The king's questions went on for a long time; I wondered whether I would ever have an opportunity to answer him. Finally he sat back and awaited my presentation. His manner was imperious; he had a sneer on his face that said he was prepared to reject everything I had to say to him. He turned with a grin to one of his aides as if to say, "This is going to be entertaining. Let's see what wild stories this crazy old wandering Hebrew has for us." He was a man accustomed to deference from a craven corps of followers; he was a bully with a loud voice and a commanding personality, surrounded by people hoping for his favor and fearful of his rejection. How could I survive this interview?

On the other hand, he had sent for me – I had not requested this meeting. Perhaps beneath all that bluster was a kernel of concern; perhaps he was less sure of himself than he seemed. I had known such personalities and finally found the courage to deliver my message of pending doom to a man who might strike me down in an instant.

—⚏—

XI

Jonah Before the King

As I began to speak, the sun was high in the western sky. By the time I finished my presentation, the sky had turned black.

"O king of this great city, Nineveh, I come neither as spy nor as enemy but as a messenger of warning to you and to your people," I began.

"I did not choose to come here. Indeed, I resisted the word of the Lord that came to me for I feared for my safety. Because my message is filled with doom and dread for you and your people, I was sure you would reject the message and kill me. So I ran from the Lord but He overtook me and cast me deep into the sea for many days until I was content to bow to His will and bring His message to this great city.

"For there is one God, and he is a great and powerful Lord who rules the sea and the dry land. He cannot be denied. I speak of the one great God whom you know not, whom you deny in your ignorance. Instead you have chosen for yourselves your own gods of wood and stone who are powerless to speak or to do anything to save you from the wrath of a just and powerful Lord who will no longer be denied."

My audience was quiet now but I could feel agitation among these godless listeners. I was encouraged to go on despite an air of menace in the room.

"But who am I that I should speak for the Lord, the Master of all that is?

"I am Jonah of Galilee, a Hebrew in the family of Abraham's descendants. Abraham was ancestor to the Hebrews and to you, the Assyrians as well, I believe.

"Many generations ago, Abraham was led by God from Ur of the Chaldeans up to Haran on the Balikh River, then on a great journey down to Damascus and Shechem, the Land of the Canaanites. There God appeared to Abraham and promised all that land to his descendants. Abraham built an altar there and worshiped the Lord, then traveled on to Bethel and into Egypt with his family and possessions, all the while being led by the Lord. For many years he traveled through the region, from Egypt back into Canaan, from Hebron to Gerar and Beersheba, increasing his flocks, family and followers as he traveled.

"God had promised Abraham many descendants, but both Abraham and his wife, Sarai, were very old. Yet Abraham believed God and it was credited to him as righteousness. In fact, two sons were born to Abraham: Isaac by his wife, Sarai, and Ishmael by Sarai's maidservant, Hagar. It is the descendants of Isaac who will possess the land promised to Abraham and we believe that Ishmael's descendants are the mighty peoples of this land, even the Assyrians of whom you are king. Ishmael, your ancestor, had 12 sons who became tribal rulers in the area from Havilah to Shur near the border of Egypt *'and they lived in hostility toward all their brothers,'* according to our ancient writings.

"Isaac, our own ancestor, followed the Lord. Isaac's son Jacob had many sons who founded the 10 tribes of the Hebrews who to this day follow the Lord with faithfulness and thanksgiving, from the eldest to the youngest. For the Lord has spoken to His people with these words:

> *"See, I am setting before you a blessing and a curse — the blessing if you obey the commands of the Lord your God; the curse if you disobey the commands of the Lord your God..."*

"I, Jonah, am the Lord's prophet to these people, the Hebrews. I am not a prophet to the Gentiles, and I have no authority here. Yet the Lord has sent me to you with a message:

> *"'Alas for that day! For the day of the Lord is near.'*

"In 40 days — now only seven days — this city will be destroyed for its depravity and corruption."

Still there was no reaction from the king and his court except for a heavy silence. Though I could hear a few grumbles and a nervous rustling in the audience, I noted that all were listening to me very closely.

"The hostility of Ishmael and his descendants has come down to you, O King. The Lord, who is a righteous God and without mercy for those who deny Him will wreak His vengeance on this city. For all your ways are an abomination in His sight. As Ezekiel warned,

"*You rely on the sword, you do detestable things, and each man defiles his neighbor's wife.*'

"I will tell you why the Lord has pronounced destruction upon the city of Ninevah:

"The Lord declares a curse on the man who lies with his father's wife, or his sister, or the daughter of his father or mother, or with his mother-in-law. Yet in your city there is no sanctity in marriage or the family. Incest is common among your people, and it is an abomination before the Lord.

'*If a man commits adultery with another man's wife, both the adulterer and the adulteress must be put to death*,' according to the Lord's command. And yet adultery is a normal practice, even a sport among your people. It is an abomination before the Lord.

"'*If a man lies with a man as one lies with a woman, both of them have done what is detestable. They must be put to death,*' says the Lord. Yet in your city this detestable practice is celebrated among the people. It is an abomination before the Lord.

"He declares a curse on any who pervert justice, especially on the stranger in your city, or the fatherless or the widow. Yet there is no justice in your courts for any of these, nor for your own citizens who for a bribe will testify against their neighbors, while the judge who will decide their complaint will favor the one with the greater bribe. This, too, is an abomination before the Lord.

"He has declared a curse upon any one who smites his neighbor secretly. But in your society no member is safe who is weaker than his neighbor. As I walk through your streets I see all around me a people bracing themselves against the next attack or assault; their eyes will not meet; no one trusts his neighbor and no one is secure on your streets. It is an abomination before the Lord.

"According to His laws and precepts, all graven images are an abomination before the Lord. The Lord declares a curse on the man who makes any graven or molten image. Yet as I walk through your city all I see are idols of wood and stone. The people drop their coins at the feet of these lifeless objects, and why? Will their gods protect them from the diseases that rage through your population from season to season? If you bow down to those objects, will they increase your power or add a single day to the span of your life, mighty King of the Assyrians?

"Let me tell you a story:

"There was a time when the Philistines of Ashdod stole the ark of the covenant of the Lord, the most precious evidence of the presence of the Lord among His people, the Hebrews. The Philistines tried to set it up against their idol Dagan. The next morning they found Dagan face down in the dirt before the ark of the Lord. They set Dagan up again but on the second morning Dagan's hands and feet had been severed from its body and the people of Ashdod became grievously ill. In their panic they tried to remove the ark from their presence but when they laid hands upon it the illness spread and they became afflicted with terrible bodily tumors. The outcry of those people was heard in heaven but their god, Ashdod, was silent.

"Your graven images, King of the Assyrians, will serve your people no better than did Ashdod to the aid of the Philistines.

"The practices of your priests are an abomination before the Lord for they practice divination and sorcery; they interpret omens and engage in witchcraft and cast spells; they are mediums and spiritists who would consult the dead. Anyone who does these things is detestable to the Lord! I challenged your priests the other day. 'Appeal to your false gods,' I said. 'Let us see if your images in wood and stone can stand against the will of the one true Lord.'

"I have not heard since from your priests!

"I am sure you are aware that the merchants of your city conspire against each other. Are you aware of their conspiracy against you as well, hiding the profit from their enterprise in order to avoid your taxes while paying expensive bribes to your agents for favoritism? There is no respect for your rule, only fear because your hand is heavy upon the people. They don't love you – they hate you. And when the Lord moves against your city your people will quickly abandon you. And the Lord will surely move against you very soon with a terrible wrath!

'He will stretch out His hand against you and make you a desolate waste.'"

As I left the king's presence, I was trembling from my boldness though I was unrestrained by the members of his court as I left the hall. They seemed to be in shock as though stunned by my words while a morbid stillness settled over the company. I returned to my lodgings satisfied that I had discharged the responsibility with which the Lord had charged me; I could know with a clear conscience that as the city crumbled before my eyes I had done all I could to warn every level of institution, from the lowliest citizen on the street to their king on his throne.

—⚏—

XII

A Royal Decree

The day after my interview with the king I arose early to see what effect, if any, my words might have had. I was astonished at what I found.

With only six days remaining until Nineveh was to be destroyed, the king had sent out a proclamation to the citizens of Nineveh:

"Do not let any man or beast, herd or flock, taste anything; do not let them eat or drink. But let man and beast be covered with sackcloth. Let everyone call urgently on God. Let them give up their evil ways and their violence. Who knows? God may relent and with compassion turn from His fierce anger so that we will not perish."

Posters were mounted in all the public gathering places. Heralds called out the king's orders. Every household received the message and was required to acknowledge the royal decree. Each citizen of the city was directed to participate in a general act of penance with fasting and public mourning. All the usual routines of the city were to come to an abrupt halt while people fell to their knees with pleas for mercy before a vengeful God.

There was to be no eating or drinking for six days. All meetings and public functions were to be cancelled. Schools were to be closed. Everyone, even the sick and the crippled, was to appear in the streets for a collective show of grief for the sins of Nineveh. The king and his court, especially, would kneel with the people in ashes, clothed with rags. Even the beasts must suffer without food or water so that their misery would be added to that of the people. Perhaps God would spare them if He could be persuaded of their repentance, they prayed.

I was gratified at the power of my preaching, but I was also concerned that God might, in His mercy, forgive them. I fell on my knees with a recitation of the evils of this city and a call for God's severest judgment. These people deserve the promised destruction, I cried, all the while fearing what the outcome might be for Nineveh.

—❧—

XIII

The 40th Day

On the morning of the 40th day since the beginning of my holy assignment I rose early hoping to view the destruction of the great city of
Nineveh. I had left the city the night before and was camped on a hilltop,
seated beneath a shady arbor I had fashioned out of a wild grapevine. It was
my intention to witness the city's destruction from this vantage point. I did not
know how the Lord would carry out His pronouncement. Would it be fire and
destruction from above? An earthquake, perhaps? Or was some pitiless army
crouching outside the city gates, prepared to lay ruin to the whole hateful rabble
and royalty of Nineveh? I waited with a sick anticipation, dreading the sight of
such wholesale suffering while reveling in the justice about to be brought upon
this sinful populace by a vengeful God.

I waited all day. But no destruction appeared. The 40 days had passed. The
city's pleas for mercy and confessions of sin before God's law had been heard.
They would be spared, just as I had feared.

I was thrown into a pious and self-righteous rage. I fell to the ground and
showered my head with dirt and dust, crying out my lament to God:

"O Lord, is this not what I said when I was still at home? That is why I was
so quick to flee to Tarshish. I knew that you are a gracious and compassionate
God, slow to anger and abounding in love, a God who relents from sending
calamity. Now, O Lord, take away my life, for I would rather die than live!"

In my rage I went back to sit beneath my shelter to watch the city, all day
and the following night. As the sun rose the next morning I discovered that
during the night the vines had dried and shriveled. There was no more shelter

from a blazing sun and scorching east wind. I was miserable. Not only must I accept the survival of Nineveh and the repudiation of all my pronouncements, but it seemed that God was punishing me with the ferocity of sun and wind. I cursed the vine and more than ever I wanted to die. In self-pity, I cried out to the Lord.

The answer came to me as clearly as though God stood before me there, on the outskirts of Nineveh.

> *"You have been concerned about this vine though you did not tend it or make it grow. It sprang up overnight and died overnight. But Nineveh has more than a hundred and twenty thousand people who cannot tell their right hand from their left, and many cattle as well. Should I not be concerned about that great city?"*

I considered these words in shame. I realized that had I drowned in the sea, Nineveh, too, would have perished. But God, in His mercy, saved my life; and He preserved the lives of the people of Nineveh as though theirs were of a value equal to my own.

—⚏—

Epilogue

The book of *Jonah* was not written so we might marvel at the power of God to bring a man back to life after three days in the belly of a whale. We see a similar miracle every time a child is born after nine months in the water of the womb.

The message of *Jonah* is God's patience and love for His creation. The popular image of God as an angry, avenging tyrant is belied by this story in which God is shown to have a more forgiving nature than a man. He has compassion for even the lowliest: those *"who cannot tell their right hand from their left."*

Jonah was chagrined to discover God's love in contrast to his own self-righteous judgment. God was prepared to forgive whereas Jonah wanted a terrible verdict of destruction. And so Jonah cursed the withered vine, a metaphor for his own definition of justice. In the end, it was Jonah who was judged.

God does not defer judgment forever, however. The Old Testament book titled *Nahum*, thought to have been written 100 years after *Jonah*, foretells the eventual destruction of Nineveh. Nahum says,

> *"The Lord is slow to anger and great in power;*
> *The Lord will not leave the guilty unpunished."*

And,

> *"He cares for those who trust Him,*
> *but with an overwhelming flood*
> *He will make an end of Nineveh."*

And,

> *"An attacker advances against you, Nineveh.*
> *Guard the fortress,*
> *watch the road,*
> *brace yourselves,*
> *marshal all your strength."*

Repentance saved Nineveh during Jonah's time but the corporate memory is short and repentance is not inheritable from generation to generation. The Assyrians returned to idolatry and an orgy of pillage of their neighbors, making themselves rich with plunder. Evidence of the ferocity and splendor of the reigns of the Assyrian Kings Sennacherib and Ashurbanipal was unearthed in 19th century archeological explorations. Among the accumulated wealth of the Assyrians were found remnants of the wisdom of that age, including scholarship on astrology, literature, law and medicine that had been stolen from surrounding peoples and brought to Nineveh. All their wealth and learning, however, failed to protect the Ninevites from the onslaught of a coalition of Medes and Babylonians, who destroyed Nineveh in 612 B.C.

About the Author

Robert W. Foster is a retired civil engineer. He was graduated from the University of Vermont in 1955 and served in the United States Air Force where he completed pilot training in 1958. He practiced as a consulting engineer in the Framingham, Massachusetts area until his semi-retirement in 1992. In retirement, he continues to provide consulting services in construction review, provides dispute-resolution services and writes frequently for technical publications. He served as president of the *Federation Interationale de Geometre* from 1998 to 2002. He has three sons and two grandsons. His wife of 47 years, Margot, died in 2001. He lives in Hopkinton, Massachusetts.

—✺—

www.ingramcontent.com/pod-product-compliance
Lightning Source LLC
Chambersburg PA
CBHW070337290526
45791CB00003B/1374